LET'S LEARN SOMETHING NEW!

Use at least 11 of your spelling words in a short creative story. Underline all spelling words used in the story.

Spelling Test

Your Answers	Correct Spelling If Incorrect
1	1
2	2
3	3
4	4
5	5
6	6
7	7
8	8
9	9
10	10
11	11
12	12
13	13
14	14
15	15
16	16
17	17
18	18
19	19
20	20

6th Grade Extra Credit Spelling Words Worksheet

Name: _____

Date: _____

anticipate	anguish	anxious	abandon	appeal	apprehensive
apparel	abundant	ambition			

. NOAABND   _ _ _ n _ o _

. ANUDTANB   a _ _ _ _ _ _ t

. MABITOIN   _ m b _ _ _ _ _

. ISNHUAG   _ n _ u _ _ _

. TIETCNAIPA   a _ _ i _ _ _ _ t _

. SUXOAIN   _ _ _ i _ _ s

. RALAEPP   a _ _ _ r _ _

. PAPEAL   a _ p _ _ _

. PSRPIEVEHEAN   a _ _ r _ _ _ n _ _ _ _

Write sentences using words from above:

_____

_____

_____

_____

Use at least 9 of your spelling words in a short creative story. Underline all spelling words used in the story.

Spelling Test

Your Answers		Correct Spelling If Incorrect	
1		1	
2		2	
3		3	
4		4	
5		5	
6		6	
7		7	
8		8	
9		9	
10		10	
11		11	
12		12	
13		13	
14		14	
15		15	
16		16	
17		17	
18		18	
19		19	
20		20	

6th Grade Extra Credit Spelling Words Worksheet

Name: _____

Date: _____

beacon	boisterous	chronological	barren	capacity	beneficial
capital	campaign	blunder	burden	boycott	

. RNERAB   _ a _ _ e _

. AONEBC   _ e _ _ _ n

. ALNBFCIEEI   _ _ _ e _ i _ _ _ l

. UEBDNLR   _ _ u _ _ e _

. OISRTBUEOS   b _ _ s _ _ r _ _ _

. BOTYTCO   b _ _ c _ _ _

. BEUDNR   _ _ r d _ _

. PNAGMIAC   _ _ m _ a _ _ _

. CCPAATIY   _ _ _ a c _ _ _

0. LCPAITA   c _ _ _ _ _ l

1. HNCGOCILROOAL _ _ _ o _ o _ _ _ _ _ _ l

Write sentences using 2 words from above:

_____

_____

_____

Use at least 14 of your spelling words in a short creative story. Underline all spelling words used in the story.

Spelling Test

Your Answers	Correct Spelling If Incorrect
1	1
2	2
3	3
4	4
5	5
6	6
7	7
8	8
9	9
10	10
11	11
12	12
13	13
14	14
15	15
16	16
17	17
18	18
19	19
20	20

6th Grade Extra Credit Spelling Words Worksheet

Name: _____

Date: _____

diminish	economy	effect	eerie	discretion	efficient
dialogue	diligent	dissent	distinct	dissolve	

. GUOEALID   _ _ _ _ _ _ _ _

. NLDEIGTI   _ _ _ _ _ _ _ _

. IIISMNHD   _ _ _ _ _ _ _ _

. EDICRTISNO   _ _ _ _ _ _ _ _ _ _

. NIDETSS   _ _ _ _ _ _ _

. LEVIOSDS   _ _ _ _ _ _ _ _

7. TCTSIIND   _ _ _ _ _ _ _ _

8. NEMOYOC   _ _ _ _ _ _ _

9. ERIEE   _ _ _ _ _

10. EFFETC   _ _ _ _ _ _

11. TIEFCNEIF   _ _ _ _ _ _ _ _ _

Write sentences using 4 words from above:

_____

_____

_____

_____

Use at least 7 of your spelling words in a short creative story. Underline all spelling words used in the story.

Spelling Test

Your Answers	Correct Spelling If Incorrect
1	1
2	2
3	3
4	4
5	5
6	6
7	7
8	8
9	9
10	10
11	11
12	12
13	13
14	14
15	15
16	16
17	17
18	18
19	19
20	20

6th Grade Extra Credit Spelling Words Worksheet

Name: _____

Date: _____

futile	formulates	hostile	generate	former	hazardous
habitat	genre	hoax	factor	fuse	

. OCTFAR   f _ _ _ _ _

. ERMORF   f _ _ _ _ _

. OARESMLUTF   f _ _ _ _ _ _ _ _ _

. FSEU   f _ _ _

. ETLUIF   f _ _ _ _ _

. GRTAENEE   g _ _ _ _ _ _ _

7. GERNE   g _ _ _ _

8. TTABHIA   h _ _ _ _ _ _

9. HSURDOAAZ   h _ _ _ _ _ _ _ _

10. AHXO   h _ _ _

11. EOSTILH   h _ _ _ _ _ _

Write sentences using 4 words from above:

....

....

....

....

Use at least 8 of your spelling words in a short creative story. Underline all spelling words used in the story.

Spelling Test

Your Answers	Correct Spelling If Incorrect
1	1
2	2
3	3
4	4
5	5
6	6
7	7
8	8
9	9
10	10
11	11
12	12
13	13
14	14
15	15
16	16
17	17
18	18
19	19
20	20

6th Grade Extra Credit Spelling Words Worksheet

Name: _____

Date: _____

immense	knack	Idiom	improvises	likeness	makeshift
legislation	liberate	jovial	leisure	ignite	leeway
majority					

. IDIMO   _ d _ _ _

. INEGIT   i _ _ i _ _

. NSIEMEM   i _ _ e _ _ _

. SREMPOVIIS   _ _ _ r _ v _ s _ _

. JLIAVO   _ _ v i _ _

. CKAKN   _ n _ _ _

. WYELAE   l _ _ w _ _

8. SNEOGLALTII   _ _ _ _ s _ a _ _ _ n

9. ESREUIL   _ _ _ _ _ r e

10. AREIEBTL   _ _ b _ r _ _ _

11. EKESISNL   _ _ k _ _ _ s _

12. JTAIMRYO   m _ _ _ _ i _ _

13. ISMEFHKAT   m _ _ _ s _ _ _ _

rite sentences using 4 words from above:

_____

_____

_____

_____

Use at least 12 of your spelling words in a short creative story. Underline all spelling words used in the story.

Spelling Test

Your Answers		Correct Spelling If Incorrect	
1		1	
2		2	
3		3	
4		4	
5		5	
6		6	
7		7	
8		8	
9		9	
10		10	
11		11	
12		12	
13		13	
14		14	
15		15	
16		16	
17		17	
18		18	
19		19	
20		20	

6th Grade Extra Credit Spelling Words Worksheet

Name: _____

Date: _____

| plummet | refuge | onset | quest | parody | obstacle |
| painstaking | persecute | optimist | objective | paraphrase | |

. TJBVCOEIE _ _ j _ _ _ i _ _

. BOTCEASL o _ _ _ _ _ l _

. SNTOE o _ _ _ _

. SPOITITM _ _ t _ _ _ _ t

. KSIINGATPNA _ a _ _ _ _ _ _ _ n g

. ERPAAHSRAP _ a _ _ _ _ _ a s _

7. RDAYPO _ _ _ _ d y

8. RTSECEEPU _ e _ _ _ _ _ _ e

9. MUETPML _ _ _ _ _ _ e t

10. STUEQ _ _ e _ _

11. ERGEFU r e _ _ _ _

Write sentences using 4 words from above:

_____

_____

_____

_____

Use at least 10 of your spelling words in a short creative story. Underline all spelling words used in the story.

_____

_____

_____

_____

_____

_____

_____

_____

_____

_____

_____

_____

_____

_____

_____

_____

_____

_____

_____

Spelling Test

Your Answers

1
2
3
4
5
6
7
8
9
10
11
12
13
14
15
16
17
18
19
20

Correct Spelling If Incorrect

1
2
3
4
5
6
7
8
9
10
11
12
13
14
15
16
17
18
19
20

6th Grade Extra Credit Spelling Words Worksheet

Name: _____

Date: _____

significant	rural	stationary	soothe	retrieve	sanctuary
salvage	strive	rigorous	stifle	siege	solar

. EREVETIR _ _ _ _ _ _ _

. GROIUOSR _ _ _ _ _ _ _ _

. ARRUL _ _ _ _ _

. LSAEAVG _ _ _ _ _ _ _

. NRATAYCUS _ _ _ _ _ _ _ _ _

. EIGES _ _ _ _ _

7. GINCTIIANFS _ _ _ _ _ _ _ _ _ _ _

8. SRLOA _ _ _ _ _

9. OSHTOE _ _ _ _ _ _

10. ITNOSTAYAR _ _ _ _ _ _ _ _ _ _

11. SLIEFT _ _ _ _ _ _

12. ISTRVE _ _ _ _ _ _

Write sentences using 4 words from above:

....

....

....

....

Use at least 5 of your spelling words in a short creative story. Underline all spelling words used in the story.

Spelling Test

Your Answers	Correct Spelling If Incorrect
1	1
2	2
3	3
4	4
5	5
6	6
7	7
8	8
9	9
10	10
11	11
12	12
13	13
14	14
15	15
16	16
17	17
18	18
19	19
20	20

6th Grade Extra Credit Spelling Words Worksheet

Name: _____

Date: _____

subordinate	unique	trait	superior	tangible	subsequent
terminate	terrain	swarm	supplement	transform	

. SBIRNDAOUET _ _ _ _ _ _ _ _ _ _ _

. SEEBUUNQST _ _ _ _ _ _ _ _ _ _

. UPEIRSOR _ _ _ _ _ _ _ _

. SLEPETMNPU _ _ _ _ _ _ _ _ _ _

. MRWAS _ _ _ _ _

. ABLINGET _ _ _ _ _ _ _ _

7. TENITERAM _ _ _ _ _ _ _ _ _

8. RIRENAT _ _ _ _ _ _ _

9. TTRIA _ _ _ _ _

10. RFNMSRATO _ _ _ _ _ _ _ _ _

11. EQNIUU _ _ _ _ _ _

rite sentences using 4 words from above:

_____

_____

_____

_____

Use at least 16 of your spelling words in a short creative story. Underline all spelling words used in the story.

Spelling Test

Your Answers	Correct Spelling If Incorrect
1	1
2	2
3	3
4	4
5	5
6	6
7	7
8	8
9	9
10	10
11	11
12	12
13	13
14	14
15	15
16	16
17	17
18	18
19	19
20	20

Use at least 14 of your spelling words in a short creative story. Underline all spelling words used in the story.

Spelling Test

Your Answers	Correct Spelling If Incorrect
1	1
2	2
3	3
4	4
5	5
6	6
7	7
8	8
9	9
10	10
11	11
12	12
13	13
14	14
15	15
16	16
17	17
18	18
19	19
20	20

Use at least 17 of your spelling words in a short creative story. Underline all spelling words used in the story.

Spelling Test

Your Answers		Correct Spelling If Incorrect	
1		1	
2		2	
3		3	
4		4	
5		5	
6		6	
7		7	
8		8	
9		9	
10		10	
11		11	
12		12	
13		13	
14		14	
15		15	
16		16	
17		17	
18		18	
19		19	
20		20	

Use at least 5 of your spelling words in a short creative story. Underline all spelling words used in the story.

_____

_____

_____

_____

_____

_____

_____

_____

_____

_____

_____

_____

_____

_____

_____

_____

_____

_____

_____

_____

Spelling Test

Your Answers	Correct Spelling If Incorrect
1	1
2	2
3	3
4	4
5	5
6	6
7	7
8	8
9	9
10	10
11	11
12	12
13	13
14	14
15	15
16	16
17	17
18	18
19	19
20	20

Use at least 7 of your spelling words in a short creative story. Underline all spelling words used in the story.

_____

_____

_____

_____

_____

_____

_____

_____

_____

_____

_____

_____

_____

_____

_____

_____

_____

_____

_____

Spelling Test

Your Answers	Correct Spelling If Incorrect
1	1
2	2
3	3
4	4
5	5
6	6
7	7
8	8
9	9
10	10
11	11
12	12
13	13
14	14
15	15
16	16
17	17
18	18
19	19
20	20

Use at least 12 of your spelling words in a short creative story. Underline
all spelling words used in the story.

Spelling Test

Your Answers	Correct Spelling If Incorrect
1	1
2	2
3	3
4	4
5	5
6	6
7	7
8	8
9	9
10	10
11	11
12	12
13	13
14	14
15	15
16	16
17	17
18	18
19	19
20	20

Use at least 10 of your spelling words in a short creative story. Underline all spelling words used in the story.

Spelling Test

Your Answers	Correct Spelling If Incorrect
1	1
2	2
3	3
4	4
5	5
6	6
7	7
8	8
9	9
10	10
11	11
12	12
13	13
14	14
15	15
16	16
17	17
18	18
19	19
20	20

Use at least 8 of your spelling words in a short creative story. Underline all spelling words used in the story.

Spelling Test

Your Answers	Correct Spelling If Incorrect
1	1
2	2
3	3
4	4
5	5
6	6
7	7
8	8
9	9
10	10
11	11
12	12
13	13
14	14
15	15
16	16
17	17
18	18
19	19
20	20

Use at least 13 of your spelling words in a short creative story. Underline all spelling words used in the story.

Spelling Test

Your Answers	Correct Spelling If Incorrect
1	1
2	2
3	3
4	4
5	5
6	6
7	7
8	8
9	9
10	10
11	11
12	12
13	13
14	14
15	15
16	16
17	17
18	18
19	19
20	20

Use at least 11 of your spelling words in a short creative story. Underline all spelling words used in the story.

_____

_____

_____

_____

_____

_____

_____

_____

_____

_____

_____

_____

_____

_____

_____

_____

_____

_____

Spelling Test

Your Answers	Correct Spelling If Incorrect
1	1
2	2
3	3
4	4
5	5
6	6
7	7
8	8
9	9
10	10
11	11
12	12
13	13
14	14
15	15
16	16
17	17
18	18
19	19
20	20

Use at least 9 of your spelling words in a short creative story. Underline all spelling words used in the story.

Spelling Test

Your Answers		**Correct Spelling If Incorrect**	
1		1	
2		2	
3		3	
4		4	
5		5	
6		6	
7		7	
8		8	
9		9	
10		10	
11		11	
12		12	
13		13	
14		14	
15		15	
16		16	
17		17	
18		18	
19		19	
20		20	

Use at least 15 of your spelling words in a short creative story. Underline all spelling words used in the story.

Use at least 11 of your spelling words in a short creative story. Underline all spelling words used in the story.

Spelling Test

Your Answers	Correct Spelling If Incorrect
1	1
2	2
3	3
4	4
5	5
6	6
7	7
8	8
9	9
10	10
11	11
12	12
13	13
14	14
15	15
16	16
17	17
18	18
19	19
20	20

Use at least 9 of your spelling words in a short creative story. Underline all spelling words used in the story.

Spelling Test

Your Answers		Correct Spelling If Incorrect	
1		1	
2		2	
3		3	
4		4	
5		5	
6		6	
7		7	
8		8	
9		9	
10		10	
11		11	
12		12	
13		13	
14		14	
15		15	
16		16	
17		17	
18		18	
19		19	
20		20	

Use at least 14 of your spelling words in a short creative story. Underline all spelling words used in the story.

_____

_____

_____

_____

_____

_____

_____

_____

_____

_____

_____

_____

_____

_____

_____

_____

_____

_____

_____

_____

Spelling Test

Your Answers	Correct Spelling If Incorrect
1	1
2	2
3	3
4	4
5	5
6	6
7	7
8	8
9	9
10	10
11	11
12	12
13	13
14	14
15	15
16	16
17	17
18	18
19	19
20	20

Class: _____

		Week or Month:_____					Week or Month:_____					Week or Month:_____					Week or Month:_____				
Day																						
Date																						
Assignments																						
Name																						
	1																					
	2																					
	3																					
	4																					
	5																					
	6																					
	7																					
	8																					
	9																					
	10																					
	11																					
	12																					
	13																					
	14																					
	15																					
	16																					
	17																					
	18																					
	19																					
	20																					
	21																					
	22																					
	23																					
	24																					
	25																					
	26																					
	27																					
	28																					
	29																					
	30																					
	31																					
	32																					

Class: _____

		Week or Month:_____				Week or Month:_____				Week or Month:_____				Week or Month:_____			
Day																		
Date																		
Assignments																		
Name																		
	1																	
	2																	
	3																	
	4																	
	5																	
	6																	
	7																	
	8																	
	9																	
	10																	
	11																	
	12																	
	13																	
	14																	
	15																	
	16																	
	17																	
	18																	
	19																	
	20																	
	21																	
	22																	
	23																	
	24																	
	25																	
	26																	
	27																	
	28																	
	29																	
	30																	
	31																	
	32																	

Made in the USA
Monee, IL
12 February 2021